CLOSER TO GOD
Bible Studies

Philippians

SIXTEEN LESSONS FOR INDIVIDUALS,
ONE-ON-ONES, AND SMALL GROUPS

BARB RAVELING

Scripture quotations are from The ESV® Bible (The Holy Bible, English Standard Version®), copyright © 2001 by Crossway, a publishing ministry of Good News Publishers. Used by permission. All rights reserved.

Cover Design by Cindy Kiple

Interior Design by Cindy Kiple

ISBN 979-8-9893557-0-9

Contents

Introduction

Have you ever sat down to read your Bible and thought, *I just don't feel that close to God?* I felt that way on and off for twenty-five years. I loved God, and I *wanted* to feel close to Him, but it wasn't happening. That all changed when I started going to God for help with my problems more than twenty years ago.

Not only did God give me insight through His Word and truths that helped me see my struggles in a different light, He also embraced me in His loving arms. I felt His presence and grew to love my time with Him. I'm hoping this Bible study will do the same for you.

ABOUT THE SERIES

I call the series Closer to God Bible Studies because these Bible studies are all about drawing closer to God as you go to Him for help with your day-to-day struggles, habits, temptations, and trials.

Each day you'll look at a small section of Scripture, and I'll provide questions you can use to apply the passage to something that's going on in your life right now. It may be something you've been struggling with for a long time, something small that happened yesterday, or something that's not even on your radar right now—but it will be after this Bible study!

I'm hoping you'll use the questions to cozy up into God's lap and talk over your problems with Him. At the end of each study, I'll give you a prayer suggestion, then ask you to identify your biggest takeaway.

The term *takeaway* is one we use in life coaching. It means, what was your aha moment? Where did the Holy Spirit give you insight or pour out truth? Often, I'll learn a new insight just by answering that question.

I'll also ask if you'd like to take any action steps based on that day's lesson. Try to make the action steps practical and specific. For example, you might write "Record five things I'm thankful for each day" or "Call Jo and apologize for what I said to her yesterday" or "Leave my phone in the kitchen unless I need it to call someone" or "Do a Google search to see how other Christians deal with this issue."

While it's helpful to ask and answer this question, don't be alarmed if you can't follow through on all your action steps. Paul talks about so many different topics in this book that every lesson could be a new project—and it's impossible to change everything at once!

So go ahead and answer the question, work on what you can do now, but don't stress if you can't do everything. In doing this study with my husband and some of our friends, I found that it's helpful for growth even if we can't change everything at once.

ABOUT THE STUDY

One purpose of Bible study is to know God's Word and what it means. To fulfill that purpose, we study the Greek and Hebrew meanings of words and look at other passages that tie in with the passage we're reading. This helps us to get to know the Word, and I love Bible studies like that.

But another purpose of Bible study is to take in the truth of God's Word and apply it to our lives so we can grow in holiness. That's what this Bible study is about. Instead of having Greek and Hebrew definitions and lots of questions about the passage itself and related Bible verses, I'll ask questions to help you apply the passage to a current struggle you're facing.

It might be a recurring temptation, a big trial, a relationship issue, an ongoing work problem, or something that just started bothering you. Use the Bible passage to understand your situation and brainstorm ways to deal with it based on the Scripture. I'll provide questions to walk you through the process.

I begin each lesson with this instruction: Summarize or diagram this passage. Use this in whatever way works best for you to learn the essence of the Bible passage. I've included the main Scripture passage in each lesson, which will make it easier to answer the questions, but you'll also need a Bible to look up additional references.

Following is an example of how my husband, Scott, and I summarized James 5:12–15. You can see that they're very different because of our personalities and what we focused on in the passage.

> *But above all, my brothers* and sisters, *do not swear, either by heaven or by earth or with any other oath; but your yes is to be yes, and your no, no, so that you do not fall under judgment. Is anyone among you suffering?* Then *he must pray. Is anyone cheerful? He is to sing praises. Is anyone among you sick?* Then *he must call for the elders of the church and they are to pray over him, anointing him with oil in the name of the Lord.*

Barb's diagram:

- Don't swear by heaven or earth → yes be yes and no be no.
- Suffering → Pray
- Cheerful → Sing praises
- Sick → Call the elders of the church to pray over you and anoint you with oil
- Prayer of faith → restores the one who is sick → the Lord will raise him up. If he's committed sins, they'll be forgiven him.

Scott's summary:

- Don't make promises you can't keep.
- Don't be wishy-washy.
- Pray, pray, and pray.

Do you see how different our summaries are? I diagram and Scott summarizes. When Scott summarizes a passage, he's looking for the bottom line. When I diagram a passage, I'm looking for relationships—if/then (for example: if you're suffering, then pray), command/promise, etc. I also look for guiding principles, definitions, characteristics of God, different ways to love well, or anything else that strikes my eye. Do whatever will help you learn the essence of the passage. If you'd like to see more examples of diagramming a passage, check out this resource: barbraveling.com/how-to-diagram-scripture.

ABOUT PHILIPPIANS

Before we begin, let's take a quick look at the book we'll be studying. Philippians was written by the apostle Paul around AD 61 to the church in Philippi. Paul had visited the Philippians at least two times, possibly more, on missionary trips, so he had a good relationship with them and a fondness for them.

More interesting than who it was written to, though, is where Paul wrote the letter. He wrote it from prison! This is intriguing because one of the biggest themes in Philippians is how to be content when life is hard. Paul talks about rejoicing always, dwelling on the good, and learning to be content in any situation. These are lessons Paul would have had ample opportunity to learn given his current living conditions. We often think we need certain things to be happy, but Paul, writing from prison, teaches us that, no, we can be content in any situation. This is just one of the many valuable lessons we'll learn in this Bible study.

INDIVIDUALS, ONE-ON-ONES, AND SMALL GROUPS

This study is an effective tool for individuals, one-on-ones (two people), or small groups if the members know one another well or want to know the others better. Because some of the questions are personal, it's most useful for groups in which participants are willing to open up to one another and also for people who welcome growth. It can lead to great discussions as the lessons cover topics we all struggle with.

If you're doing the study by yourself, use it as a time to commune with God and go to Him for help with life. Each lesson covers a different topic, and some topics may affect you more deeply than others. If that happens, you may want to take several days to explore the topic with some of the action steps you listed before you move on to the next lesson.

Because we'll use this study to work on transformation, you may be tempted to beat yourself up when you see your shortcomings through the eyes of the Bible passage. If you're tempted to do that, remember that *all* of us struggle with sin and weakness and that God is a God of grace (Romans 3:23; 7:15–20; Hebrews 4:14–16). Beating ourselves up is fruitless, but going to God for help with transformation is life-changing.

This is also a great study for one-on-ones since it deals with real-life issues. It could be used with a friend, family member, or in a mentoring relationship, such as a mentor/mentee, campus ministry leader/student, or youth group leader/student. If you use this book to mentor someone, I suggest both of you do the studies individually each week, and then meet to share what you learned.

Philippians works well for a group study as each lesson covers a completely different topic. Normally, Bible studies are directed toward a certain age group, but because this study is mostly made up of questions, it can be used with any age. I've had readers write and tell me they used *James* (my first Bible study in this series) with their young married group, their eighty to ninety-year-old group, their women's church study, and even as a Bible study for a grandma and her two granddaughters. It can also be a great resource for a youth or college group to help them work through the challenges that come with those stages of life.

 ## LEADING A GROUP STUDY

To lead a group study, ask the participants to do the studies on their own, then go through the questions one by one when you meet. If you find after the first couple of classes that you never get to all the questions (this was true for my group), choose ahead of time the questions you want to cover. One question we always included was "What is your biggest takeaway?" as it was interesting to see how God worked differently in each of our lives through that week's study.

If you don't have sixteen weeks for your class, you can do the study with the following options: 1) Choose the lessons you want to cover, still doing one per week, and let class members do others on their own. Because each lesson covers a completely different topic, this is a workable solution; 2) let each group member choose one or two lessons they'd like to discuss and just do those lessons; or 3) assign more than one lesson per week and discuss the highlights of each lesson as you won't have time for a full discussion. You could do that by asking these questions: What stood out to you in this lesson? What challenged you most? What was your biggest takeaway? This may not lead to as deep of a discussion (which is why this would be my least favorite option), but it would allow you to cover more lessons.

Since a couple of personal questions are included in each study, be sensitive when asking how individuals answered them. Let class members decide whether or not to share personal details. Also, be careful that one person doesn't take over the discussion each week by sharing all of their troubles related to the lesson! (You can find ideas for what to do in a situation like this by Googling "Bible study members who talk too much.")

Always be loving and gentle, recognizing that people are at different points in their walks with God and they have different personalities. While one class member might be willing to share everything in her life, another class member will have a hard time sharing personal things. That's okay. There are still many opportunities for growth from both the group discussions and doing the lessons alone with God.

My prayer is that this study will lead to many wonderful times with God and opportunities to go to Him for help with your daily struggles—and also wonderful times of deep fellowship with others if you do it with a group or another person. May God bless you through the study of His Word!

ONE

When You Feel Like a Failure

PHILIPPIANS 1:1–8

1 Paul and Timothy, servants of Christ Jesus, To all the saints in Christ Jesus who are at Philippi, with the overseers and deacons: 2 Grace to you and peace from God our Father and the Lord Jesus Christ. 3 I thank my God in all my remembrance of you, 4 always in every prayer of mine for you all making my prayer with joy, 5 because of your partnership in the gospel from the first day until now. 6 And I am sure of this, that he who began a good work in you will bring it to completion at the day of Jesus Christ. 7 It is right for me to feel this way about you all, because I hold you in my heart, for you are all partakers with me of grace, both in my imprisonment and in the defense and confirmation of the gospel. 8 For God is my witness, how I yearn for you all with the affection of Christ Jesus.

OBSERVE

1. Summarize or diagram this passage. (See Introduction for an explanation of how to do this. If you'd rather just record notes as you read the passage or draw an image that helps you understand the passage better, that works too!)

THINK

2. In verses 3–4, Paul says that he always thanks God when he remembers the Philippians and prays for them with joy. According to this passage, what are some reasons we can pray for our Christian loved ones with thankfulness and joy?

One reason we can pray for our Christian loved ones with joy is because we have the assurance that God will finish what He has begun in them (Philippians 1:6). This verse also brings *us* joy when we're praying that God would change some area of our lives, but we don't see Him answering that prayer yet. Because the rest of this passage is mostly a greeting to the Philippians, I'd like to focus today's lesson on verse 6.

3. List a few things you've tried to change but just can't seem to make it happen. It might be a recurring sin, a habit you'd like to start or stop, or an emotion you struggle with such as worry, anger, or insecurity. It could also be an area of weakness you think God might like you to address such as developing better work habits or limiting the time you spend on your phone. List a few of those things now, then choose one of them to work on for this lesson.

4. If you could change that area of your life with the snap of your fingers, what would your life look like after the change?

We all have different strategies or ways we approach change based on our personalities and previous life experiences. We may barrel straight ahead doing everything we can to change, or we may sit back because it seems like too much work to change—or we feel like we can't change—or it hasn't crossed our minds to work on change in this area of our lives. Or we may plead with God to change us, get frustrated when He doesn't, and then beat ourselves up when we fail because "we should be different by now!"

5. Think of the area you mentioned in question 3. Which of the above strategies have you been using to approach change in that area of your life so far?

6. Do you think you'll change if you continue with that strategy? Why or why not?

The truth is, if we're using one of the strategies I mentioned earlier, we probably won't see change unless God decides to perform a miracle in our lives. We may think the barrel-ahead strategy works, but it only works with things we can change in our own strength (such as things we're naturally good at or a new skill we're learning). With things we *can't* change in our own strength (such as anger, anxiety, compulsive habits, etc.), we need to go to God consistently for help or we won't see transformation. Thankfully, Paul reminds us in Philippians 1:6 that He who began a good work in us will complete it. Let's see what that looks like with the concern you mentioned in question 3.

7. What do you think God would like to see happen in that area of your life?

8. Why do you think God wants that to happen?

If you have a tendency to see God as a demanding critical Father, you may have answered that last question with something like, "Because God is tired of me messing up all the time!" But here's the truth: God *loves* us. Yes, He wants us to stop sinning and grow in the areas where we're weak, but He doesn't want us to change because "we're terrible people!" Instead, He has a bigger vision of what life could be for us. Here's a bit of that vision: He wants us to live in freedom, to be wholly submitted to Him, to feel close to Him, to grow in holiness, to serve others sacrificially, and to walk in the fruit of the Spirit. And if you look at the fruit of the Spirit in Galatians 5:22–23, that's a good life!

9. It would be far easier if God would just step in and change us with the blink of his eye, but when we look at the Bible as a whole, it becomes clear that God is more like a coach than a fairy godmother when it comes to sanctification.[1] Think of what you know about fairy tales and sports teams. What's the difference between a coach and a fairy godmother?

10. What would it look like to work with God as your coach in the area you mentioned in question 3?[2]

When we make a plan to change an area of our lives that God wants us to change, we often experience defeat early on. This happens for several reasons. First, we're usually not naturally good in the areas we struggle with, so it's not surprising when we fail. Second, even though a big part of us wants to change, there's often another part of us that *doesn't* want to change because we know it will involve sacrifice. Finally, we're more likely to experience spiritual attacks at the beginning of the transformation process because that's when we're weakest and most likely to give up. When defeat and discouragement set in, it's important to go to Scripture to remember who God is in the midst of our struggle. Let's do that now.

11. Read the following Bible verses and imagine feeling defeated because you *once again* failed to change in the area you mentioned in question 3. According to the following Bible verses, how will God "coach" you through your failure if you go to Him for help rather than giving up, beating yourself up, or continuing to work on change only in your own strength?

Psalm 32:8

Psalm 37:23–24

Psalm 91:2–4

Jeremiah 31:3–4

 **PRAY**

12. When we go to God for help with transformation, He gives us wise counsel, perspective, strength, comfort, and encouragement. This helps us feel closer to Him as we rest in His loving arms. Read today's Bible passage again, then spend some time thanking God for the assurance that He will finish what He has begun in both you and your loved ones, then visit with God about partnering with Him in working on the area of your life you mentioned in question 3. You can either write your prayer in the space below or just visit with God without writing anything down.

 **TAKEAWAY**

13. What is your biggest takeaway from today's lesson?

 **ACTION STEPS**

14. List any action steps you'd like to take based on your takeaway. (See Introduction for examples of steps you could take.)

Chapter 1 Footnotes

1. In fairy tales, we see the fairy godmother wave her magic wand and change people in the blink of an eye, but we don't see God doing that with sanctification (the process of breaking free from our sins and growing in holiness) in the Bible. Think of the lives of Jonah, Moses, and David. Over and over we see them visiting with God about their struggles. God didn't do everything for them—and He expected them to change—but He was also there helping them change by discussing life with them. We also see this behavior modeled with Jesus and His disciples. Jesus healed people of physical ailments, but He didn't ever heal them from things like worry or immoral thoughts or even doubting Him. He had conversations with them about those things and encouraged them, but He didn't give them instant transformation in those areas.

2. If this question is hard to answer, check out my book The Renewing of the Mind Project, or this blog post/podcast: https://barbraveling.com/how-to-renew-your-mind/. It's also important to remember that while God coaches us, He also forgives us, comforts us, and wipes away our tears when we fail. He is the Perfect One to help us with the sanctification process.

PHILIPPIANS

TWO

Loving When It's Hard to Love

PHILIPPIANS 1:9–11

9 And it is my prayer that your love may abound more and more, with knowledge and all discernment, 10 so that you may approve what is excellent, and so be pure and blameless for the day of Christ, 11 filled with the fruit of righteousness that comes through Jesus Christ, to the glory and praise of God.

 OBSERVE

1. Summarize or diagram this passage.

 **THINK**

2. We've all heard the saying "Love is blind," but in this passage Paul is praying that the Philippians would love with eyes wide open—with a love that abounds in real knowledge and all discernment. What's the difference between a love-is-blind sort of love and a love that is growing in knowledge and discernment?

3. Some may say that the more you get to know people, the harder it is to love them because you can see their faults. Yet Paul is talking about a love that grows stronger with knowledge. How might knowing someone better (either God or people) lead to loving them better?

While it would be nice if we could stay in Growing-in-Love Land, the sad truth is that most relationships go through difficult periods in which our love seems to grow less and less rather than more and more. In those situations, we need the knowledge and discernment Paul talks about if we want our love to abound more and more. Let's see what this looks like in our own lives.

4. Who are you having a difficult time loving lately (or who have you been annoyed with)? List those people below or in your mind, then choose one person (preferably someone you know well) and answer the rest of the questions with that person in mind.

5. Why do you have a difficult time loving this person (or what is it about them that gets on your nerves)?

6. Sometimes it's easier to love people when we know their backgrounds and have some insight into why they are the way they are. Think of the person you mentioned in question 4. Think of their parents, the way they grew up, their experiences in life, their personality, and anything else that affects their behavior. Now think of this person's annoying or hurtful habits that are bothering you. Where do you think those habits are coming from? (For example, someone who was abused when they were younger may be triggered if you say something that feels like an attack, and someone who grew up in a passive family may also have a tendency toward passivity. That

doesn't mean God approves of their behavior, but it does help us understand where it's coming from.)

7. When we take the time to think of why people do the things they do, we're taking the time to get to know them better—and Paul tells us we'll grow in love as we grow in knowledge. When you think of everything you recorded in the last question, does it change your feelings toward the person you're annoyed with? In what way?

8. When I get annoyed with someone, a good honest look at my own faults (knowledge and discernment) can help me grow in love toward them. Think of a current situation you're going through with this person who annoys you. Do you have any faults that are negatively contributing to this situation? How do your faults contribute to your annoyance?

9. Now think of the way you grew up, your life experiences, your personality, and anything else that affects your behavior. Why do you think you struggle with the faults you mentioned in the last question?

10. One of the redeeming qualities about trials, including the trial of difficult relationships, is that God can use that trial to help us grow and mature in ways He wants us to grow and mature.[3] With your faults in mind, can you think of anything God might want you to learn from the annoying or hurtful behavior of this person or any ways He may want to use this situation to help you grow and mature? Be specific.[4]

11. It helps us love people when we grow in knowledge of both them and ourselves, but it also helps us love people when we grow in knowledge and discernment about how God wants us to love people. Read 1 Corinthians 13:4–7 and Matthew 7:1–5. What parts of these passages do you need to adopt to love this person well?

Paul tells us that learning to love better will lead to approving what is excellent and becoming pure and blameless, filled with the fruit of righteousness. The Greek word translated as "pure" here is *eilikrines*, and it means to be pure and unsullied with the idea of "that which is cleansed by much rolling and shaking to and fro in the sieve."[5] Difficult relationships can make us feel like we're shaking to and fro in a sieve. That shaking can lead to bitterness and resentment, or it can lead to becoming more pure and blameless.

12. What would you need to do in this situation to experience cleansing and growth rather than bitterness and resentment?

 **PRAY**

13. Read today's Bible passage again, then visit with God about the person who annoys you and also about how your own faults contribute to the situation. Ask God for wisdom, discernment, and direction for how to respond to this person and this situation. You can either write your prayer in the space below or visit with God without writing anything down.

TAKEAWAY

14. What is your biggest takeaway from today's lesson?

ACTION STEPS

15. List any action steps you'd like to take based on your takeaway. (See Introduction for examples of steps you could take.)

Chapter 2 Footnotes

3. See also James 1:2–4 and Romans 5:3–5.

4. God always has things to teach us through difficult relationships, but sometimes the lesson He wants to teach us is to stop people pleasing or living in fear and be a bit more assertive. (Moses getting the Israelites out of Egypt and Abigail in 1 Samuel 25 are both examples of this type of love.) If you're in an abusive relationship, please get help as soon as possible.

5. See interlinear tab for Philippians 1:9 on BlueLetterBible.org, eilikrines, Strong's 1506 entry, Trench's synonyms LXXXV: eilikrines, katharos.

THREE

Making Life About God

PHILIPPIANS 1:12–20

12 I want you to know, brothers, that what has happened to me has really served to advance the gospel, 13 so that it has become known throughout the whole imperial guard and to all the rest that my imprisonment is for Christ. 14 And most of the brothers, having become confident in the Lord by my imprisonment, are much more bold to speak the word without fear. 15 Some indeed preach Christ from envy and rivalry, but others from good will. 16 The latter do it out of love, knowing that I am put here for the defense of the gospel. 17 The former proclaim Christ out of selfish ambition, not sincerely but thinking to afflict me in my imprisonment. 18 What then? Only that in every way, whether in pretense or in truth, Christ is proclaimed, and in that I rejoice. Yes, and I will rejoice, 19 for I know that through your prayers and the help of the Spirit of Jesus Christ this will turn out for my deliverance, 20 as it is my eager expectation and hope that I will not be at all ashamed, but that with full courage now as always Christ will be honored in my body, whether by life or by death.

OBSERVE

1. Summarize or diagram this passage.

THINK

2. In this passage, Paul talks a bit about his experience in prison. In Paul's time, people could be thrown in jail for preaching the Word of God, and that's where Paul is as he writes his letter to the Philippians. My guess is that you probably aren't in danger of being arrested for your faith. But have you ever been in situations where you didn't want to share your faith or let others know you're a Christian because you were afraid people would judge or reject you? Explain.

3. It seems strange to me that Paul's imprisonment encouraged other believers to speak the Word of God with boldness. You would think that his imprisonment would make them even more fearful because they wouldn't want to go to prison. What is the likely negative out-

come for you if you speak up in the situations you mentioned in the previous question?

4. When we tell others we're Christians, or tell them about God, we have a potentially good outcome and a potentially bad outcome. We talked about the possible bad outcome. What is a possible good outcome?

5. Paul also talks about competition in ministry in today's Bible passage (v. 15). We've all experienced this as it's easy to look around and feel envious or less-than when we compare ourselves with others. Are you currently envious of anyone in the same ministry or vocation[6] as you? If so, what do they have that you don't have? (If you can't think of anyone in your vocation or ministry that you envy, think of someone else you envy.)

The interesting thing is that envy is often a two-way street. We might be envious of others over something they have, but they may be envious of us for something we have. For example, in today's passage Paul's contemporaries were jealous of Paul's success in ministry, yet Paul could easily have been envious of them because he was in prison and they weren't!

6. Choose one of the people you mentioned in question 5. Is there anything *you* have that they don't have? List those things.

Thinking about our blessings helps us let go of envy, but another way to let go of envy is to make life about God and be satisfied with Him alone. Paul could have sat in prison dwelling on the unfairness of the situation, but instead, Paul was just thankful his contemporaries were preaching Christ, even if their motives weren't pure. For Paul, life was about God—not about being top dog in ministry (Philippians 1:18, 21; 3:8)—and because of that, he wasn't envious of his peers.

7. Now think of the person you envy. What are you tempted to make life about in that situation? (For example, Paul's contemporaries were making life about success in ministry. We're often tempted to make life about comfort, financial security, travel, relationships, popularity, or any number of things.)

When we make life about things other than God, it's easy to get depressed when we don't get enough of what we want. Because Paul was more concerned about bringing glory to God rather than bringing glory to himself, it was easier for him to rejoice in prison, even though prison life wasn't easy. Let's see how this works in our own lives.

8. List two or three hard things you're going through right now, then choose one to work on for the rest of the questions.

9. What outcome are you hoping for in your trial, and why do you want that outcome?

10. If you were to switch your *main* desired outcome to living in fellowship with God and keeping Him first in your life (Matthew 6:33; Luke 10:38–42), how would that affect your attitude and actions?

11. At the beginning of this passage, Paul says his circumstances have served to advance the gospel. That's still happening today as we read Paul's letters and apply the wisdom he learned through his trials to our own lives. Can you think of any ways your current trial could advance the gospel? If not, can you think of any lessons God wants to teach you through this trial?

12. When you think about how God wants to use your trial for good, how does it make you feel?

 PRAY

13. Read the passage again with your trial in mind. Ask God to strengthen you, comfort you, and help you to keep His interests at the forefront of your mind as you go through this trial, trusting in Him rather than in the positive outcome you desire.

 **TAKEAWAY**

14. What is your biggest takeaway from today's lesson?

 ACTION STEPS

15. List any action steps you'd like to take based on your takeaway.

Chapter 3 Footnotes

6. See the first two paragraphs in Lesson 10 for clarification of what I mean by vocation.

FOUR

Letting Go of Idols

PHILIPPIANS 1:21–26

21 For to me to live is Christ, and to die is gain. 22 If I am to live in the flesh, that means fruitful labor for me. Yet which I shall choose I cannot tell. 23 I am hard pressed between the two. My desire is to depart and be with Christ, for that is far better. 24 But to remain in the flesh is more necessary on your account. 25 Convinced of this, I know that I will remain and continue with you all, for your progress and joy in the faith, 26 so that in me you may have ample cause to glory in Christ Jesus, because of my coming to you again.

 OBSERVE

1. Summarize or diagram this passage.

THINK

2. Paul begins this section by saying, "For to me to live is Christ, and to die is gain." List all the advantages of living that Paul gives (written or implied).

3. List the advantages of dying that Paul gives (written or implied).

4. Why do you suppose Paul thought the "stay" option was better, when his desire was to go and be with Christ? (Remember, Paul is writing this letter from prison, so it's not like he had a perfect life at the moment.)

5. Paul lived for Christ, but we often live for other things. When we start caring for those other things more than God, they become idols in our lives. These idols keep us from being able to say with Paul, "To live is Christ, to die is gain." To help discover what your idols may be, answer the following questions:

a. What do you feel you have to have to be happy?

b. What do you wake up in the middle of the night thinking of?[7]

6. If a and b in question 5 are very different, what do you think the relationship is between the two? What needs are you trying to fill with each one?

7. Does your pursuit of (or longing for) the things you mentioned in the previous two questions interfere with developing such a close walk with Jesus that you really *do* feel like life is about Him (v. 21)? Explain.

8. If you look back at the things you want in question 5, my guess is that most of them are good things—or at least not bad things. At what point does something you love become an idol?

9. For me, good things become idols when I feel like I have to have them to be happy or I start relying on them more than God for safety and security. The funny thing is that I think I can get enough of those things to be happy and safe. Let's see if this is true. Look back at your answers to question 5. Do you think you can get enough of those things to be happy and safe throughout your life? Why or why not?

10. The culture tells us we need certain things to be happy and safe, yet the Bible tells us that we'll never get enough of our idols to be satisfied with them. Our best chance of feeling happy and safe is to make life about God. Read the following Bible verses and record what God says about happiness and safety (either directly or indirectly).

a. Psalm 16

b. Psalm 121

c. Luke 10:38–42

d. John 16:33

e. Philippians 4:11–13

11. What would you gain if you were to reach the point where you felt like God was enough, in other words, relying on Him for happiness and safety rather than the things you mentioned in question 5?

12. What are some steps you could take on a practical level to move toward more of a life-is-about-God life?

 **PRAY**

13. Read today's Bible passage again, then ask God to help you give up your idols and develop such a close relationship with Him that you can truly say "to live is Christ." Also ask Him in what way He wants you to serve or disciple others.

TAKEAWAY

14. What is your biggest takeaway from today's lesson?

ACTION STEPS

15. List any action steps you'd like to take based on your takeaway.

Chapter 4 Footnotes

7. Often our worries indicate our idols. So if I wake up in the middle of the night worrying about finances, it could indicate that financial security is an idol. If you'd like to explore your idols more, take my idolatry quiz at https://barbraveling.com/do-you-have-an-idol-quiz/. I also have a chapter on idolatry in my Bible study *Freedom from Emotional Eating*.

FIVE

Church and Relationship Struggles

PHILIPPIANS 1:27–30; 2:1–2; 4:2–3

1:27 Only let your manner of life be worthy of the gospel of Christ, so that whether I come and see you or am absent, I may hear of you that you are standing firm in one spirit, with one mind striving side by side for the faith of the gospel, 28 and not frightened in anything by your opponents. This is a clear sign to them of their destruction, but of your salvation, and that from God. 29 For it has been granted to you that for the sake of Christ you should not only believe in him but also suffer for his sake, 30 engaged in the same conflict that you saw I had and now hear that I still have. 2:1 So if there is any encouragement in Christ, any comfort from love, any participation in the Spirit, any affection and sympathy, 2 complete my joy by being of the same mind, having the same love, being in full accord and of one mind. 4:2 I entreat Euodia and I entreat Syntyche to agree in the Lord. 3 Yes, I ask you also, true companion, help these women, who have labored side by side with me in the gospel together with Clement and the rest of my fellow workers, whose names are in the book of life.

 OBSERVE

    1. Summarize or diagram this passage. (Note: Although we usually go through the verses in order, I've included Philippians 4:2–3 with this passage since it shares the topic we'll be covering in this lesson.)

 THINK

    2. In this passage Paul emphasizes standing and serving together in one spirit. It reminds me of Jesus's last prayer in John 17:20–21 when he asked his Father to help the disciples to be united in one spirit. Why do you suppose Paul and Jesus care so much about Christians getting along with one another? (Answer for yourself first, but then look up the following verses if you need ideas: John 17:20–21; Ephesians 4:26–27, 29; Hebrews 3:12–14; 10:24–25.)

    3. Think of your own church and any squabbles that might be occurring. What will you and your fellow church members miss out on and what consequences will you experience if you don't learn to get along? See question 2 for ideas. (If you can't think of any disagreements in the church, think of an ongoing relationship you have with

another Christian that isn't always easy. What will you and this person miss out on and what consequences will you experience if you don't learn to get along?)

4. It's helpful to think about what we'll miss out on if we don't get along, but it's also helpful to think about what our community will miss out on if church members (and the churches in the community) don't get along. What roles does Jesus want the church to play in your community, and why is getting along important to accomplish those purposes?

We all want a church that feels like a safe haven, but I've attended a couple of churches where unity wasn't a prominent feature! Church quarrels start for a number of reasons, but it's often a lack of maturity on the part of leadership and/or church members that escalates minor differences into a full-blown battle. When people are angry, condemning, hateful, controlling, or gossipy, small annoyances become big problems.

At other times, though, disagreements aren't just minor annoyances. This has happened frequently in recent years as many churches have gone through significant changes in how they approach things like theology, politics, and human sexuality. People on both sides might be sincere people of faith, but still, those changes may be so big that you no longer feel comfortable at your church.

5. At what point do you think it's legitimate to leave your church and search for another?

I know of one church that changed its practice from believer baptism to infant baptism, but the congregation decided to live together in love while disagreeing (in love) in the area of baptism. That said, your church may have gone through a change you feel you can't accept. At that point, you need to pray about it and decide what to do. Now let's see what this looks like on a personal level.

6. Think of your church. List anything that is currently bothering you about the church, the people in the church, or the way the church is run. (If you can't think of anything, list some things that are bothering you about a Christian you're in an ongoing relationship with.)

7. Which of those annoyances are major issues and which ones are just a different way of doing things?

8. Sometimes we think we need to bring up every little thing that bothers us, but that can be discouraging and demoralizing to the people we're annoyed with. Other times, we really should bring something up, but because of people pleasing or passivity, we're unwilling to do so. Are you a person who tends to bring things up too often or not enough? Why might God want you to change in that area?

9. In Philippians 1:27, Paul tells us to let our manner of life be worthy of the gospel of Christ so that we can live in unity. He explains what this looks like in Colossians 3:12–17. How could you influence the church (or the person you mentioned in question 6) for good if you were to live out these verses in your relationship with them?

10. Sometimes God asks us to focus on the good (in people and the church) and learn to be content with life as-is because no church or person is perfect, including us. But other times God may want us to step in and work toward change if the leadership or other person in the relationship is open to it. At what point do you think it's worth talking to church leadership or the other person in the relationship about something you're not happy with?

11. If you do talk to someone with whom you have a conflict, what should that conversation look like in light of Colossians 3:12–17?

One of the things I love about Jesus is that He gives us grace. He forgives us when we act in a way that is unworthy of the gospel. But it doesn't stop there. He wants us to extend that same grace to others—forgiving and accepting them when they live in a way that is unworthy of the gospel (Matthew 5.43–46, 18.21–22; Romans 15:1, 7; Colossians 3:12–15).

12. What makes it so difficult to extend grace to some of the people you mentioned in today's lesson?

13. What would you have to give up or accept to be able to forgive those people and give them grace?

God always calls us to forgive and give grace, but that doesn't mean we can't put up boundaries or enact church discipline or even leave relationships if God is okay with it. Unfortunately, much of what is done in church and relationships is done in a spirit of judgment, condemnation, and self-righteousness (focusing on the faults and sins of others while ignoring our own) rather than in a spirit of love with a desire to build up and restore the other person to fellowship with God and holiness. This is one of those areas of our lives where it's helpful to visit with other wise believers and God about what to do.

 **PRAY**

14. Read today's Bible passage again, then visit with God about one of the struggles you mentioned in today's lesson. Confess any sin on your part and ask God to help you be an encourager and a uniter and give you wisdom in how to handle any disagreements in your church or relationship.

 **TAKEAWAY**

15. What was your biggest takeaway from today's lesson?

 **ACTION STEPS**

16. List any action steps you'd like to take based on your takeaway.

SIX

People Pleasing, Self-Pleasing, and God Pleasing

PHILIPPIANS 2:3–4

3 Do nothing from selfish ambition or conceit, but in humility count others more significant than yourselves. 4 Let each of you look not only to his own interests, but also to the interests of others.

OBSERVE

1. Summarize or diagram this passage.

 **THINK**

2. Paul begins this passage by telling the Philippians not to do anything from selfish ambition. Selfish ambition isn't a phrase we typically use today. Instead, when we speak of ambition, we usually think of it as positive, not negative. How would you define selfish ambition?

In this passage Paul talks about selfish ambition in the context of relationships. Relationships work best when there's a give and take, but sometimes we get "selfishly ambitious" and refuse to look out for the interests of others. Let's see what this looks like in a real-life situation.

3. Think of an ongoing relationship in which you're currently annoyed with the other person because you have different "ambitions." For example, you might want a clean house and they might want a messy house. Or you might want to talk through relationship difficulties, but they may want to avoid conversations like that. List what each of you wants below.

You

The other person

4. What would selfish ambition on your part look like in this situation?

5. How would you respond if you were to take Paul's advice and look out for the interests of your friend or loved one in this situation?

6. It's easy to read this passage and think, *Oh, we just need to give up our own needs and desires and always do what the other person wants us to do.* (See question 3.) Yet in Galatians 1:10, we find that God wants us to please Him rather than people. So, in a relationship, we have three things to consider: what I want, what the other person wants, and what God wants. How would you respond to the person you

mentioned in question 3 if you were a) people pleasing (doing what the other person wants), b) self-pleasing (doing what you want), or c) God pleasing (doing what God wants)?

People pleasing

Self-pleasing

God pleasing

Sometimes when we choose to please God, we'll annoy the other person. Other times when we please God, it will come with great sacrifice as we give up our own desires. We may not know what God wants, but it's always helpful to pray about it. God may not tell us exactly what to do, but He'll help us have a humble, loving heart as we do it.

7. Now let's look at the word *conceit* in verse 3. The Greek word used here for conceit means "glory without reason," or in today's terms, feeling like we're great when we're really *not* great! In what ways do you think you're great in this situation and the other person is terrible?

8. Often in conflict situations, we fall into the trap of thinking we're great and the other person is terrible, when in reality we both have strengths and weaknesses. Think of your current conflict. What are the other person's strengths in this situation? What are your weaknesses in this situation?

9. Verse 3 of Philippians 2 tells us to think of the other person as more significant than ourselves, but it clarifies how we are to do that: with humility. Verse 4 explains it further: Look not only to our own interests, but also to the interests of others. From a biblical perspective, what is the interest of the other person in this situation? In other words, what does *God* want for this person?

10. What attitude would you need to have and how would you need to behave for the best chance of making that happen?

11. Jesus shows us that when we look out for the interests of others, it often involves suffering on our part (Philippians 2:5–11). Jesus suffered to the point of death. If you do what you suggested in questions 6c, 10, and possibly 5 (if God also wants that), will that cause you to suffer? If so, in what ways could you suffer?[8]

Often when I sacrifice and give up things for God, I *think* I'm going to be miserable, but I end up full of joy because I've grown closer to God and more like Him through the experience. Jesus also experienced this joy. Hebrews 12:2 tells us that Jesus endured the cross for the "joy set before Him."

12. In the previous question you looked at the ways you might suffer if you please God and others and not just yourself in this situation. What are some benefits *you* might receive if you carry out this sacrificial behavior as a loving act of worship[9] to God?

PRAY

13. Read today's Bible passage again with this relationship or situation in mind, then ask God for wisdom in how He wants you to handle it.

TAKEAWAY

14. What is your biggest takeaway from today's lesson?

 **ACTION STEPS**

15. List any action steps you'd like to take based on your takeaway.

Chapter 6 Footnotes

8. If you're using this lesson to work through an abusive relationship, please get outside help as soon as possible, as it can be hard to see things clearly when you're in the midst of it.

9. Romans 12:1–2.

PHILIPPIANS

SEVEN

Loving with Jesus-Style Love

PHILIPPIANS 2:5–13

5 Have this mind among yourselves, which is yours in Christ Jesus, 6 who, though he was in the form of God, did not count equality with God a thing to be grasped, 7 but emptied himself, by taking the form of a servant, being born in the likeness of men. 8 And being found in human form, he humbled himself by becoming obedient to the point of death, even death on a cross. 9 Therefore God has highly exalted him and bestowed on him the name that is above every name, 10 so that at the name of Jesus every knee should bow, in heaven and on earth and under the earth, 11 and every tongue confess that Jesus Christ is Lord, to the glory of God the Father. 12 Therefore, my beloved, as you have always obeyed, so now, not only as in my presence but much more in my absence, work out your own salvation with fear and trembling, 13 for it is God who works in you, both to will and to work for his good pleasure.

 **OBSERVE**

1. Summarize or diagram this passage.

Paul begins today's Bible passage by encouraging the Philippians to have the same attitude Jesus had when He sacrificed on the cross for us. In the previous verse (Philippians 2:4), Paul reminded the Philippians to look out for the interests of others. When we give up our own interests to look out for the interests of others, it almost always involves sacrifice on our part. We can see this demonstrated in the life of Jesus.

THINK

2. Think of how Jesus lived and how He died during his sojourn on earth. What sacrifices did Jesus make to put the interests of others (us) before his own interests?

It's not easy to give up our own interests. That's why we need to "work out [our] salvation with fear and trembling" (Philippians 2:12).[10] Thankfully, God is at work in us both to will and to work for

His good pleasure. To will means to *want*. We start out wanting to do *our* good pleasure, but we end up wanting to do *His* good pleasure.

We see how much work it takes to give up our will and look out for the interests of others when we look at the life of Jesus. In the garden of Gethsemane, Jesus went to His Father again and again for the strength and desire to do His will. It wasn't easy, but that time with His Father led to His others-centered actions in Philippians 2:6–8. Let's see what this might look like in our lives.

3. Begin by listing three of your faults that get in the way of looking out for the interests of others. (Some examples include spending too much time on your phone, working too much or not enough, talking too much or not enough, being passive or controlling, having a critical spirit, or yelling at people. Only include faults that interfere with loving others well.)

4. Now choose two of those faults to work on for this lesson. If you were to look out for your own interests with each of those faults, what interests would that be? (For example, if I spend too much time on my phone, I might be looking out for my interests of satisfying my curiosity, being entertained, escaping life, or avoiding what I *should* be doing.)

Fault #1

Fault #2

5. If you were to "work out your salvation with fear and trembling," looking out for God's interests and the interests of others rather than your own, how would your attitude and behavior change in each of those areas? (For example, if I'm looking out for God's interests and the interests of others, I'll be more intentional about how I use my time. Instead of using my phone whenever I feel like it, I'll create boundaries so it doesn't get in the way of doing things God wants me to. Then I'll use that time I free up to spend time with God, serve others in ways God wants me to serve, pursue deep relationships, work, rest, and rejuvenate with fun activities).

Fault #1

Fault #2

6. How would your new attitude and behavior lead to accomplishing God's purposes in the lives of yourself and others? Be specific.

7. Just as Jesus had to make sacrifices to look out for our interests, we also need to make sacrifices to look out for the interests of others. What sacrifices might you need to make to follow through with what you suggested?

8. Imagine yourself five years down the road. Let's say you've changed in these areas and your new life is quite different because of those changes. Do you think you would enjoy your new life more or less than you do now? Explain.

9. What truths do you need to remember to be content embracing this new life? (For example, if I'm working on spending less time on my phone, I need to embrace the truth that my phone use isn't a "neutral" activity. Instead, the amount of time I spend on my phone affects my work, relationships, mental health, opportunities to serve, and even how close I feel to God and others. I also need to realize that my life is *better* with phone boundaries and that God wants me to change in this area.)

10. List some things you can look forward to as you lean on Jesus to live a life of sacrificing to love others well. (See also Matthew 25:23; John 14:1–4; Philippians 3:7–8; and James 1:2–4.)

 PRAY

11. Read today's passage again, then visit with God about the changes you considered in question 5. Ask Him which of those areas, if any, He'd like you to work on, and ask Him for wisdom and strength to begin that work.

TAKEAWAY

12. What is your biggest takeaway from today's lesson?

ACTION STEPS

13. List any action steps you'd like to take based on your takeaway.

Chapter 7 Footnotes

10 I like what David Guzak said about this verse: "We know that Paul did not mean 'work so as to earn your own salvation.' Such a statement would contradict the whole of Paul's gospel. What Paul did mean is to call the Philippians to put forth real effort into their Christian lives." (David Guzik, "Study Guide for Philippians 2 by David Guzik," Blue Letter Bible. Last Modified 6/2022. https://www.blueletterbible.org/comm/guzik_david/study-guide/philippians/philippians-2.cfm.)

EIGHT

From Complaining to Contentment

PHILIPPIANS 2:14–15

14 Do all things without grumbling or disputing, 15 that you may be blameless and innocent, children of God without blemish in the midst of a crooked and twisted generation, among whom you shine as lights in the world.

OBSERVE

1. Summarize or diagram this passage.

 **THINK**

2. In this passage, Paul mentioned four things he wanted the Philippians to be: blameless, innocent, without blemish, and lights in the world. He also mentioned two things that got in the way of that: grumbling and disputing. We'll discuss grumbling in this lesson and disputing in the next lesson. How would you define *grumbling*?

3. I would guess most of us grumble at times. We may complain about what's happening in the world, the weather, annoying people, and even our own shortcomings, such as how inept we are at things we'd like to be better at. What do you tend to complain about, either silently or out loud?

The Bible's instructions aren't random. Instead, God has them there specifically to tell us how He wants us to live. He knows that when we do the dos (be kind, forgive, etc.), it helps us and others, and when we do the don'ts (don't envy, don't complain, etc.), it hurts us and others. Let's see how this plays out with the "don't" of do not grumble.

4. Choose one or two of the grumbles you mentioned in the previous question and describe how complaining about each of those things hurts the following:

You

The people who listen to you complain (and your relationships with them)

Your testimony (aka your ability to be a light in the world)

Often I grumble about things when what I really need to do is either take action or let go and trust God. For example, I may grumble about feeling overwhelmed, when what I need to do is evaluate my work and life to see what I need to eliminate (or delegate) so I can stop feeling overwhelmed. Or I may grumble about a person who spends hours complaining to me when I should instead have a conversation with them, or if that hasn't worked in the past, put up some boundaries so I don't listen to hours of complaints. Or I may grumble about things I can't change when what I need to do is to let go, trust God, and learn how to live the best life possible in the context of what I can't change.

5. Think of the grumbles you mentioned in question 4. Do you think God wants you to take action, let go and trust Him, or a combo of the two?

6. If God wants you to take action, what might that be? Brainstorm some ideas.

It's helpful to identify action steps we can take, but it's just as important to look at what we need to accept and let go of. For example, if I'm complaining about how inept I am at getting things done, not only do I need to work on time management, but I also need to accept that I'm not a Type A person and cling to the biblical truths that He who began a good work in me will complete it and I can do all things through Him who strengthens me![11]

If I'm complaining about a loved one who is often critical, not only do I need to work on seeing myself through God's eyes rather than the eyes of my critical loved one, but I also need to accept the fact that this is who my loved one is, and because of that, he or she will criticize me.[12] This recognition will help me not take the criticism personally and not try to please a person whom I can never completely please. It will also help if I remember the biblical truth that we *all* have faults (Romans 3:23), and I also have faults that keep me from loving my critical loved one well.

7. Think of the grumbles you mentioned in question 4. If God wants you to let go and trust Him, what would you need to accept and what biblical truth would you need to cling to in order to do that?

8. In addition to replacing complaining with action, letting go, and trusting God, we can also replace complaining with focusing on the good in life and people and being thankful. Choose one of the grumbles you mentioned in question 4 and list five good things about that person or situation that you can praise God for. (If you can't think of anything, list five things you can be thankful for about who God is in that situation.)

9. If you were to develop a habit of thanksgiving and dwelling on the good, how would it affect the following:

Your tendency to grumble, either out loud or to yourself

Your personal well-being

The people who listen to you complain (and your relationships with them)

Your testimony (aka your ability to be a light in the world)

PRAY

10. Read today's passage again and visit with God about any grumbles that came up in today's lesson. Ask Him for wisdom, compassion, and the strength to change anything He wants you to change about the way you do life and relationships.

TAKEAWAY
11. What is your biggest takeaway from today's lesson?

ACTION STEPS
12. List any action steps you'd like to take based on your takeaway.

Chapter 8 Footnotes

11. Philippians 1:6; 4:13.

12. It might also help to have a conversation with our critical loved one, but that doesn't mean our loved one will immediately change. After all, we know from experience how hard it is to change our faults and it's also hard for other people to change their faults!

NINE

Loving Well When You Disagree

PHILIPPIANS 2:14–16

14 Do all things without grumbling or disputing, 15 that you may be blameless and innocent, children of God without blemish in the midst of a crooked and twisted generation, among whom you shine as lights in the world, 16 holding fast to the word of life, so that in the day of Christ I may be proud that I did not run in vain or labor in vain.

OBSERVE

1. Summarize or diagram this passage.

 **THINK**

2. In the previous lesson we looked at the grumbling part of these verses. In this lesson we'll focus on disputing. Let's begin by looking at what else the Bible has to say about disputes. Read the following verses and record what they say about disputes.

Proverbs 15:1

2 Timothy 2:23–25

Romans 14:19

3. In the previous lesson we talked about how the dos and don'ts of the Bible have a purpose. Based on these Bible verses, what end results are the writers of these verses looking for when they tell us not to argue? (See Philippians 2:15 and Romans 14:19.)

4. I've been in many helpful discussions in which people disagreed with me. I needed to hear what they said because I had to change the way I either thought or did things. But I've also been in unhelpful discussions that just made me mad at others or they at me. At what point does a discussion go from being helpful to build people up (Romans 14:19) to harmful and divisive (2 Timothy 2:23–24 and Titus 3:9)?

I can see why Paul included grumbling and disputing in the same sentence because our grumbles often lead to disputes. For example, if I'm silently grumbling about people who believe differently than I do in the political arena, I'll be more likely to argue politics with them.

5. Look back at your list of grumbles in question 3 of the previous lesson. Which of those grumbles causes you to argue with people? List those below. Also list anyone in your life you often argue with and what you argue about.

When we argue, we're often trying to change someone's beliefs or actions because we think their beliefs or actions will hurt them, us, others, or the world at large in some way. Let's see what this looks like with our tendencies to argue.

6. Choose one of the people you mentioned in question 5. Who (or what) do you think they'll hurt if they don't change their beliefs or actions, and what are you hoping to achieve (or avoid) by trying to get them to change their beliefs or actions? (If you're not trying to change their beliefs or actions but are arguing because you like to argue or because that's your go-to when people disagree with you, does your arguing help or hurt your relationship with this person? Explain.)

7. Now recall your arguments or discussions with this person. How are you usually thinking of them during the conversation? Are you lifting them up in your mind as a creation (or child) of God who believes or acts differently than you do? Or are you thinking of them as a know-nothing nitwit who will destroy you, themselves, the ones you love, or the world at large with their far-fetched ideas? Be specific as to how you are seeing them.

8. When you see this person the way you mentioned in question 7, how does that affect your relationship with them?

9. Is that a true picture of who this person is? Also, is that how God sees them? Explain.

10. If you wanted to pursue a Romans 14:19 relationship with this person, how would you need to change the way you approach your discussions and disagreements with them?

11. Would you be more likely or less likely to get them to change their opinion in an argument if you approached the discussion with a Romans 14:19 (and a 1 Corinthians 13:4–8) attitude? Explain.

12. Do you think God would rather have you stop discussing the topics you often argue about with this person or change the way you discuss those topics with both your words and attitude? Why does He want you to take that approach?

Sometimes we need to stop saying things that lead to arguing, but other times we need to speak up a bit more and be willing to engage in an uncomfortable discussion.

13. Can you think of any situations or relationships in which God may want you to speak up more than you currently do? What are you hoping to avoid or accomplish by not speaking up?

14. What might God want to accomplish by having you speak up?

PRAY

15. Read today's passage again and spend some time visiting with God about any disputes that came up in today's lesson. Ask Him for wisdom, compassion, and the strength to change anything He wants you to change about the way you do life and relationships.

TAKEAWAY

16. What is your biggest takeaway from today's lesson?

ACTION STEPS

17. List any action steps you'd like to take based on your takeaway.

TEN

Embracing Your Vocation

PHILIPPIANS 2:17–3:1

17 Even if I am to be poured out as a drink offering upon the sacrificial offering of your faith, I am glad and rejoice with you all. 18 Likewise you also should be glad and rejoice with me. 19 I hope in the Lord Jesus to send Timothy to you soon, so that I too may be cheered by news of you. 20 For I have no one like him, who will be genuinely concerned for your welfare. 21 For they all seek their own interests, not those of Jesus Christ. 22 But you know Timothy's proven worth, how as a son with a father he has served with me in the gospel. 23 I hope therefore to send him just as soon as I see how it will go with me, 24 and I trust in the Lord that shortly I myself will come also. 25 I have thought it necessary to send to you Epaphroditus my brother and fellow worker and fellow soldier, and your messenger and minister to my need, 26 for he has been longing for you all and has been distressed because you heard that he was ill. 27 Indeed he was ill, near to death. But God had mercy on him, and not only on him but on me also, lest I should have sorrow upon sorrow. 28 I am the more eager to send him, therefore, that you may rejoice at seeing him again, and that I may be less anxious. 29 So receive him in the Lord with all joy, and honor such men, 30 for he nearly died for the work of Christ, risking his life to complete what was lacking in your service to me.

 **OBSERVE**

1. Summarize or diagram this passage.

It can be difficult to diagram a passage like this because there are so many things going on. One theme I see, though, is sacrificial service. You may not have a formal ministry as Paul, Timothy, and Epaphroditus did, but you still have opportunities to serve others. One way we serve others is through our vocations—the way we spend our days. My current vocation is writing and podcasting, but in the past, I was a student, a banker, a stay-at-home mom, and a homeschool mom. At some point, I'll be a retired person.

Some vocations are service oriented so it's easy to see how we serve others in those vocations, but even with non-service vocations we have an opportunity to serve others through our relationships with the people we work with and also through the income we provide to people who depend on us.

 THINK

2. What is your current vocation, and how are you currently serving or ministering to others in your vocation?[13]

While our vocations give us numerous opportunities to serve, we also serve others outside of our vocations. Sometimes that serving takes place in significant relationships such as the things we do for our family, friends, neighbors, and other loved ones.

For example, if you're a parent with kids in the home, much of your time is spent serving your kids even if you have a day job. You serve them by reading to them at night, actively engaging in conversation with them, not letting them play computer games all night, and giving them chores to do (so they'll learn to be responsible and others-centered adults).

Like Paul, Timothy, and Epaphroditus, serving others in various relationships often involves sacrifice—we do things we don't feel like doing to love others well. We can also serve others in organized ways such as leading a Bible study or volunteering at Meals on Wheels or some other organization.

3. List the ways you serve others outside of your vocation.

4. Paul talks about being willing to sacrifice for those we serve. Are you the sort of person who tends to not serve enough or a person who serves so much that you don't have time for anything else, including your loved ones? Explain.

5. If you don't serve enough, can you think of any new areas you could begin serving in, or any people in your life you could serve a bit more, such as a spouse, family member, or a person in need of help? Brainstorm some possibilities. If you're a person who serves too much (or who always feels overwhelmed because you have too much to do), do you think God may want you to change anything in this area? Explain.

In today's passage, Paul mentions both the joys and sacrifices of serving others through ministry (v. 17).[14] Paul loved proclaiming Christ and discipling people, but he experienced real sacrifices to do so (2 Corinthians 11:23–29). In like manner, there are things we naturally enjoy in our areas of service as well as things we don't enjoy. Thankfully, most of us don't risk being stoned or beaten for doing ministry as Paul did, but we still make sacrifices to serve others well.

Let's see how this plays out in our lives. For the rest of this lesson, answer the questions with your current vocation in mind. (If you're already feeling good about your vocation, answer the questions with a relationship from questions 3 or 5 in mind. If those relationships are going well, then answer the questions with another area of service or potential service in mind from questions 3 or 5.)

6. List the vocation or relationship you'll be working on for this lesson. What do you enjoy about this vocation or relationship?

While it's helpful to focus on what we enjoy in our vocations and relationships, it's also important to recognize what we don't enjoy about them. These are the sacrifices we make to serve others. For example, as a writer, I enjoy brainstorming new books, trying out the Bible studies I write, and helping people grow, but I don't enjoy editing, decision making, and risking condemnation as I put myself out in the public eye.

When I was a stay-at-home mom, I loved going on walks with my kids, reading to them, and visiting with them, but it was a sacrifice to cook, clean, and miss out on the excitement of the workplace. If you work for someone else, you may love your work but hate how much time it takes out of your day. Or you may love visiting with the people at work but hate the drudgery of the job itself.

7. What do you *not* enjoy about your vocation or relationship?

Sometimes sacrifice is just part of the job, but other times we're sacrificing things God doesn't want us to sacrifice. For example, I may spend too much time writing because I want to produce perfect books so no one will condemn me. This would be a sacrifice since I don't love writing. God, on the other hand, may want me to *stop* sacrificing, pursue excellence rather than perfection, and use that extra time to create more resources to help people.[15]

Or I may be a homemaker who is doing all the household chores when God may want me to stop sacrificing and delegate those chores to the kids. Or I may be a people pleaser who sacrifices by working long hours at work to make the boss happy, while God might want me to either find a different job or start saying no more often if that's a possibility.

8. Look back at what you wrote in question 7. Do you see any sacrifices you're making that God may want you to stop making? If so, what do you think He wants you to do instead? (If you tend to shy away from sacrificing, can you think of any ways God wants you to *start* sacrificing to love others well in your vocation or relationship?)

When we have to sacrifice for our vocations and relationships, it's easy to start feeling sorry for ourselves. We forget that sacrifice is a necessary part of life and that everyone out there is facing the same types of sacrifices. We'll enjoy our vocations and relationships far more when we have realistic expectations for the sacrifices we might encounter along the way.

For example, I used to think people who loved to write had an easy time writing. Because I wasn't a person who loved writing, I felt sorry for myself. I started enjoying writing more when I realized *no one* enjoys everything about writing and even people who love to write often procrastinate writing. When I was a banker, I felt sorry for myself because I had to work forty hours a week. I was just coming out of sixteen years of school and felt like life should be easy!

9. Are you currently a) expecting your vocation or relationship to be easy and to be able to do it *without* having to sacrifice or b) expecting to do more than you can realistically do (or more than God wants you to do)? Explain.

10. How is your expectation (question 9) affecting your attitude toward your vocation or relationship?

11. How would it change things if you *expected* your vocation or relationship to be difficult at times, stopped trying to do more than you can realistically do (or God wants you to do), and instead ask God what *He* wants you to do, then go to Him and others for help with doing it?

It's easy to focus our vocations and relationships on what we're getting out of them (in terms of enjoyment, accomplishment, financial reward, etc.) or on meeting the needs of others. But it's intriguing to think that not only do we and others have interests in our vocations and relationships—God also has an interest! There are things He would like to see happen in both us and the people we engage with in our vocations and relationships.

For example, as a Christian writer, God wants me to create resources that will help people mature in their character and grow closer to Him. As a banker, God wanted me to love my coworkers and customers well and save money that would help when I quit work to stay home with the kids.

And in both of those vocations, God wanted me to grow in character through the trials that came with that vocation (James 1:2–4), stay close to Him during the temptations of that vocation, learn the skills necessary to do well in that vocation, and join or develop a close community of fellow believers so we could encourage and build one another up during that season of life.

12. What do you think God's interests are in your current vocation or relationship?

13. Based on God's interests, is there anything He might want you to change about the way you approach your vocation or relationship?

14. When we focus only on our own interests (or the interests of others if we're people pleasers), we rarely get enough out of our vocations and relationships to satisfy us. What would you gain if you were to start focusing more on God's interests as you minister to others through your vocation or relationship?

 **PRAY**

15. Spend some time visiting with God about the difficulties you're experiencing in your vocation or relationship. Ask Him to give you comfort, wisdom, strength, and a desire to love others well within this vocation or relationship.

 **TAKEAWAY**

16. What is your biggest takeaway from today's lesson?

 **ACTION STEPS**

17. List any action steps you'd like to take based on your takeaway.

Chapter 10 Footnotes

13. If you're retired (or in a similar situation), it may be difficult to answer this question as retirement doesn't give us specific ways to serve like a job does. What retirement does give, though, is an abundance of time to serve others in various ways.

14. Today's passage is more of a narrative of what's going on in the church rather than a passage telling us how to serve. If you'd like more help about serving, check out these verses: Matthew 20:25–28; John 15:12–17; Romans 12:9–21; Galatians 5:13–15; 1 Peter 4:8–11.

15. God also wants me to recognize that not only is it impossible to write perfect books, it's also impossible to avoid condemnation as a Christian writer. We will *all* be condemned at times but that's an opportunity to grow closer to God as we run to Him for refuge.

ELEVEN

Finding Your Identity in Christ

PHILIPPIANS 3:1–9

3:1 Finally, my brothers, rejoice in the Lord. To write the same things to you is no trouble to me and is safe for you. 2 Look out for the dogs, look out for the evildoers, look out for those who mutilate the flesh. 3 For we are the circumcision, who worship by the Spirit of God and glory in Christ Jesus and put no confidence in the flesh— 4 though I myself have reason for confidence in the flesh also. If anyone else thinks he has reason for confidence in the flesh, I have more: 5 circumcised on the eighth day, of the people of Israel, of the tribe of Benjamin, a Hebrew of Hebrews; as to the law, a Pharisee; 6 as to zeal, a persecutor of the church; as to righteousness under the law, blameless. 7 But whatever gain I had, I counted as loss for the sake of Christ. 8 Indeed, I count everything as loss because of the surpassing worth of knowing Christ Jesus my Lord. For his sake I have suffered the loss of all things and count them as rubbish, in order that I may gain Christ 9 and be found in him, not having a righteousness of my own that comes from the law, but that which comes through faith in Christ, the righteousness from God that depends on faith.

 **OBSERVE**

1. Summarize or diagram this passage.

 **THINK**

2. In this passage Paul lists all the reasons he could put confidence in the flesh if he wanted to. List those reasons.

It seems like each denomination and era of Christianity has its own version of the "good believer" list. Paul's list (vv. 5–6) is quite different from our list today or the church's list thirty years ago. Throughout the years, this list has included things like don't drink, don't dance, don't play cards, go on a mission trip each year, and volunteer at your local homeless center. I think of this as the "Good Christian List." It's the list that unofficially tells us if we're good Christians or not.

PHILIPPIANS

3. What is the current Good Christian List in your church? Or, more importantly, what's the Good Christian List[16] that's roaming around inside of your head?

4. Paul's list was all about the church because he was immersed in the church, and probably grew up in a religious family that was immersed in the church—but some of us grew up in families that weren't wrapped up in the church. Think of the family you grew up in. If they were to make a list of things you had to do or not do to be successful, what would be on the list?

5. Now think of your current life. What is on your mental list of who you need to be or what you need to do to be a successful person?

6. Now let's go back to Paul. What changed about how Paul evaluated his own righteousness? (See also Romans 7:14–8:17.)

Often, we joyfully embrace our new identity in Christ when we become Christians. But as we continue to struggle with sin and a failure to measure up to our "success list," we get discouraged and forget about our new identity in Christ. Instead of seeing ourselves through God's eyes and rejoicing in *Him* (Philippians 3:1), we see ourselves through the eyes of one of those lists we looked at in questions 3–5.

7. Which list are you currently looking at, and how is that list making you feel?

8. How do you think God feels when He sees you basing your identity and happiness on how well you accomplish that list?

9. If God were your all-loving and wise dad (which He is), what advice do you think He'd give you?

10. What would you gain if you stopped basing your righteousness, happiness, and security on the items you listed in question 7 and instead base it solely on the "surpassing worth of knowing Christ" (v. 8) and the "righteousness from God that depends on faith" (v. 9)?

While we'd all love to embrace our identity in Christ and always see ourselves through His eyes of love and grace, this is easier said than done! If you struggle with self-condemnation, feeling inadequate, and comparing yourself with others, consider working through some of the insecurity questions and Bible verses in my book *The Renewing of the Mind Project* or my *I Deserve a Donut* app. These are helpful resources whenever you find yourself beating yourself up or feeling inadequate because you're basing your identity on something other than the righteousness from God that depends on faith.

 **PRAY**

11. Reread today's passage, then visit with God about the various lists you've tried to follow all your life. Thank Him for loving you unconditionally and ask Him to help you let go of that list so you might gain Him.

 TAKEAWAY

12. What is your biggest takeaway from today's lesson?

 ACTION STEPS

13. List any action steps you'd like to take based on your takeaway.

Chapter 11 Footnotes

16. If you've always gone to churches that are heavy on grace (and low on sanctification) and you don't tend to condemn yourself, you may not have a Good Christian List roaming inside of your head.

TWELVE

Growing in Holiness

PHILIPPIANS 3:10–16

10 That I may know him and the power of his resurrection, and may share his sufferings, becoming like him in his death, 11 that by any means possible I may attain the resurrection from the dead. 12 Not that I have already obtained this or am already perfect, but I press on to make it my own, because Christ Jesus has made me his own. 13 Brothers, I do not consider that I have made it my own. But one thing I do: forgetting what lies behind and straining forward to what lies ahead, 14 I press on toward the goal for the prize of the upward call of God in Christ Jesus. 15 Let those of us who are mature think this way, and if in anything you think otherwise, God will reveal that also to you. 16 Only let us hold true to what we have attained.

 OBSERVE

1. Summarize or diagram this passage.

 **THINK**

2. Paul begins this passage by referencing two things he hasn't obtained yet. What are they? (Philippians 3:11–12)

It's interesting that one of Paul's goals is sanctification (becoming perfect), but he's not pursuing it to look good in the eyes of others. Instead, he's pursuing sanctification with the end goal of seeing God face to face and delighting in Him (v. 14). God wants us to grow in holiness (1 Peter 1:15–16), but we don't always make it a priority.

There are many reasons we don't pursue sanctification. Often, we don't feel it's that important. Instead, we focus on the truth that God loves us despite our sins, so we minimize the need to work on breaking free from our sins. Or we may think, *Well, I don't have any* huge *sins, so I think I'm good enough.* Or we may not realize how our sins are affecting others, so we don't understand the importance of working on them.

At other times, we do realize the importance of pursuing sanctification. We want to be holy, but when we try working on the sin in our lives, we experience failure. Not just once, but over and over. This discourages us and makes us want to give up the fight.

3. Think of your own relationship with sanctification. Are you a person who tends to work on becoming more holy or not work on it? If you don't work on it that much, what are the reasons you don't work on it? If you do work on it, how do you respond when you experience failure?

4. If we're saved by grace, why do you think God wants us to grow in holiness? List as many reasons as possible.

One reason God wants us to grow in holiness is so that we're equipped to love and serve others well in our current relationships and vocations. Growing in holiness involves both a taking off and a putting on (Ephesians 4:22–24).

In a relationship, we take off things like resentment, self-centeredness, people pleasing, and apathy, and we put on things like dwelling on the good in people, building them up with our words, and being proactive in discussing and dealing with conflict (or getting outside help and counseling when necessary).

In a vocation, we take off things like procrastination, perfectionism, complaining (either silently or out loud), and a what's-in-it-for-me mindset. We put on things like having a servant's heart, using our time well, becoming better at the skills needed in our vocation, and focusing on the things God wants us to focus on.

5. Think of a relationship you're currently struggling with. What do you need to take off and what do you need to put on to love that person well?[17]

6. Now think of your current vocation (see Lesson 10). What do you need to take off and what do you need to put on to serve others well in your current vocation?

7. If you were to grow in the areas you mentioned in the previous two questions, how would it affect the following?

Loving others well within that relationship and vocation

Enjoying that relationship and vocation

Your relationship with God

Representing God's character well to others

8. When we think of sanctification, it's easy to start beating ourselves up over how *un*sanctified we are and for things we've done in the past. What advice does Paul give us concerning this tendency in verse 13?

Often, we fail to move forward because we're too busy looking backward at what we did wrong in the past. God wants us to confess our sins, but He doesn't want us to beat ourselves up over them (John 8:1–11, Romans 8:1). It helps to remember that Jesus died to save us because He *knew* we weren't capable of being perfect!

When we pursue sanctification, we approach it from an already saved position. Our secure position should lead to thankfulness and a desire to grow and be all that God wants us to be so we can love others well, do whatever God has called us to do, represent His character better to others, and live an abundant life—because the holier we are, the happier we are.

9. What is one step you could take to grow in one of the areas you mentioned in questions 5 and 6?[18]

 **PRAY**

10. Read today's passage again and ask God to help you grow in holiness in general and also for specific help in the area you mentioned in the previous question.

TAKEAWAY

11. What is your biggest takeaway from today's lesson?

ACTION STEPS

12. List any action steps you'd like to take based on your takeaway.

Chapter 12 Footnotes

17 Remember that you can only control yourself in a relationship; you can't control the other person. They may be willing to work on change, but not always. If you're answering this question with an abusive relationship in mind, please get outside help as it can be hard to see things clearly when you're in the midst of the relationship.

18. In my book *The Renewing of the Mind Project*, I mention that sanctification is a partnership in which we renew our minds (Romans 12:2) and God does the transforming. If you'd like to pursue sanctification in some area of your life, this book will help.

THIRTEEN

Overcoming Temptation

PHILIPPIANS 3:17–4:1

17 Brothers, join in imitating me, and keep your eyes on those who walk according to the example you have in us. 18 For many, of whom I have often told you and now tell you even with tears, walk as enemies of the cross of Christ. 19 Their end is destruction, their god is their belly, and they glory in their shame, with minds set on earthly things. 20 But our citizenship is in heaven, and from it we await a Savior, the Lord Jesus Christ, 21 who will transform our lowly body to be like his glorious body, by the power that enables him even to subject all things to himself. 4:1 Therefore, my brothers, whom I love and long for, my joy and crown, stand firm thus in the Lord, my beloved.

OBSERVE

1. Summarize or diagram this passage.

 **THINK**

2. In this passage Paul describes two groups of people—those who walk like Paul walks and those who don't. What are the characteristics of the group who doesn't?

This passage reminds me of 1 John 2:15–17, where John talks about the lust of the flesh, the lust of the eyes, and the pride of life. "Their god is their belly" talks about the lust of the flesh.[19] "They set their minds on earthly things" reminds me of the lust of the eyes and "They glory in their shame" is similar to the pride of life.

Lust of the flesh includes things our bodies crave for instant pleasure, excitement, or escape. Spending hours on our phones, Netflix, reading novels, and playing computer games come to mind as well as overindulging in food, alcohol, and drugs.

Lust of the eyes includes things we see (often on Instagram) that we feel we *need* to have for a good life, such as better vacations, a nicer home, secure finances, a soulmate relationship, or an exciting lifestyle. The lust of the eyes is often accompanied by envy or discontentment when it's something we feel we can't get.

Pride of life is what we tend to base our identity on, such as a skinny or buff body, a prestigious job, a great girlfriend/boyfriend/spouse/kids, completing our to-do lists, or even being a great Christian. When we give into the pride of life, we're more concerned with what others think of us than what God does.

Many of the things we want in these categories are good in and of themselves. They only become the lust of the flesh, the lust of the eyes, and the pride of life when they become a means of identity, a coping technique, our main source of comfort and satisfaction, an idol, or they're sinful in and of themselves (such as pornography).

3. What do you spend too much time on, turn to for escape, rely on for identity, obsess over, or care about more than God wants you to care about it? List some of your temptations in these categories.

Lust of the flesh

Lust of the eyes

Pride of life

Circle the temptations that are currently giving you the most trouble and choose one temptation to work on for this lesson. Answer the rest of today's questions with that temptation in mind.

4. In what ways does giving in to this temptation lead to destruction (either the ultimate destruction of causing you to lose your faith or an earthly destruction of making you depressed, obsessed, broke, etc.) and make you an enemy of the cross (drawing you away from God rather than toward Him and possibly influencing others to draw away)?

Destruction

Enemy of the cross[20]

5. When we struggle with temptation, it's easy to start feeling like we'll never gain victory over it. What advice does Paul give in Philippians 4:1, and how would that be different than standing firm in your own efforts to say no to the temptation you mentioned? (Answer on your own first, but then also look up the following passages for more ideas: Matthew 4:1–11; Romans 12:2; 2 Corinthians 10:3–5; Ephesians 6:18.)

6. In verse 20, Paul reminds us that our citizenship is in heaven, where we await our Savior, Jesus Christ. He needs to remind us because so often we focus on creating a great life on earth rather than looking forward to a great life in heaven. How would shifting your focus from creating a great life on earth to looking forward to a great life in heaven affect the temptation you mentioned?

7. When we find ourselves constantly giving in to temptation, it's easy to slip into self-condemnation mode. Satan loves this because he's the accuser of the brethren (Revelation 12:10) and self-condemnation keeps us from focusing on God's power to change us. How do the following verses change your mindset when you think about going to God for help with gaining victory over your temptation?

Romans 3:23; 8:1

Ephesians 2:8–9

Romans 6:1–2

1 Peter 5:8–10

Hebrews 4:14–16

8. What is one step you think God would like you to take today to help
you stand firm in the midst of your temptation?

 **PRAY**

9. Read the passage again with your temptation in mind, then ask God for wisdom in how to handle it and the strength to stand firm.

 TAKEAWAY

10. What is your biggest takeaway from today's lesson?

 ACTION STEPS

11. List any action steps you'd like to take based on your takeaway.

Chapter 13 Footnotes

19. David Guzik explains "their god is their belly" this way: "Not that they were necessarily focused on what they eat, but belly here has a broader reference to sensual indulgence in general. They live for the pleasures of the body, mind, and soul." (David Guzik, "Study Guide for Philippians 2 by David Guzik," Blue Letter Bible. Last Modified 8/2022. https://www.blueletterbible.org/comm/guzik_david/study-guide/philippians/philippians-3.cfm.)

20. I love what Chuck Smith said about this phrase: "You know, there are a lot of people who talk a lot about Jesus Christ but are enemies of the cross of Christ. That is, they want still to live after the flesh so bad, that the idea of being crucified with Christ, the death of the old life, the death of the old man, the death of the old flesh life, is irritating to them. They don't want to hear it; they are enemies of that message. They want to tell you that you ought to be prosperous, you ought to be successful, you ought to be living in luxury, you are God's child, you ought to be indulging your flesh. Whatever you desire, just ask God, insist on God, command God. Because you can drive a Cadillac, and you can live on Lido Island. You can have these things of your flesh, you know. And it is an interesting period in church history where those who are indulging their flesh look upon it as spiritual superiority. 'You know, if you only had enough faith, you could be jetting across the United States also in your own Lear Jet.' So, it is rather tragic, because these people are opposed to the life of sacrifice, self-denial, and yet, that is the first step that Jesus said was necessary to be a disciple of His; you have got to deny yourself and take up your cross and follow Him." (Chuck Smith, "Verse by Verse Study on Philippians 3-4," Blue Letter Bible. C2000. https://www.blueletterbible.org/Comm/smith_chuck/c2000_Phl/Phl_003.cfm?a=110600.)

FOURTEEN

Praying with Thanksgiving

PHILIPPIANS 4:4–7

4 Rejoice in the Lord always; again I will say, rejoice. 5 Let your reasonableness be known to everyone. The Lord is at hand. 6 Do not be anxious about anything, but in everything by prayer and supplication with thanksgiving let your requests be made known to God. 7 And the peace of God, which surpasses all understanding, will guard your hearts and your minds in Christ Jesus.

 OBSERVE

1. Summarize or diagram this passage.

 **THINK**

2. In this passage, Paul gives us advice on how to handle anxiety (worry).[21] How would you define anxiety (worry)?

3. List three to five of your current worries.

4. Choose two of those worries to work on for this lesson. What would you like to see happen with each of those worries?

Worry #1

Worry #2

Often, we feel situations need to be resolved before we can let go of our worries and gain peace. But because Paul tells the Philippians not to be anxious about *anything*, we can assume it's possible to let go of anxiety and live in peace no matter what we're anxious about.

5. In today's Scripture reading, Paul lists five things we can do that will help us to let go of anxiety and live in peace. Let's take a minute to think about those things. How would you define each of the following?

Rejoice in the Lord (v. 4)

Be reasonable (v. 5)

Prayer (v. 6)

Supplication (v. 6)

Thanksgiving (v. 6)

6. Look back at your definitions in question 5 and your worries in question 4. How would doing all of those things lead to peace rather than anxiety?

7. Praying with thanksgiving is one of the most powerful things we can do to let go of anxiety. Let's see how this works with your current worries. For each of the worries you mentioned in question 4, list three to five things you can be thankful for within the context of that anxiety.

Worry #1

Worry #2

8. What happened when you started listing things you were thankful for?

9. Why do you think praying with thanksgiving might be more effective than praying *without* thanksgiving?

PRAY

10. Read today's Bible passage again with your worries in mind, then thank God for who He is and what He's already done in the situations you're anxious about. Also ask Him to help you make praying with thanksgiving a habit.

TAKEAWAY

11. What is your biggest takeaway from today's lesson?

ACTION STEPS

12. List any action steps you'd like to take based on your takeaway.

Chapter 14 Footnotes

21. I use the words *worry* and *anxiety* interchangeably in this lesson and the next, as they mean pretty much the same thing. Some Bible translations use the word *worry* in verse 6.

FIFTEEN

Letting Go of Anxiety

PHILIPPIANS 4:8–9

8 Finally, brothers, whatever is true, whatever is honorable, whatever is just, whatever is pure, whatever is lovely, whatever is commendable, if there is any excellence, if there is anything worthy of praise, think about these things. 9 What you have learned and received and heard and seen in me—practice these things, and the God of peace will be with you.

 OBSERVE

1. Summarize or diagram this passage.

 **THINK**

2. In this passage Paul advises the Philippians to dwell on the good, then he describes what that looks like. What happens when we dwell on the good in people and life? List as many benefits as possible.

3. The context for this passage is Philippians 4:6–7, where Paul was talking about getting rid of anxiety (worry). Think of the instances during the day when you begin worrying. What are you usually thinking about right before you get anxious? Also, are you usually dwelling on the present or the potential future? Explain.

4. Some people would say we're sticking our heads in the sand or living with rose-colored glasses if we don't worry about all the bad things that could happen in the world. What do you think Paul would say to that and why? (See also Philippians 4:6–7 and Matthew 6:25–34.)

5. Instead of worrying, God wants us to pray, and He sometimes wants us to act to prevent our worry from taking place. He also wants us to let go and trust Him.[22] Let's look at these options one at a time. Define the words and phrases below:

Worry[23]

Action

Prayer

Letting go

Trusting God

6. Now let's see what this looks like with our own worries. What are your top three current worries?

7. Of the five options I listed in question 5, what would be the best options with each of your current worries? (Note: Your worries may have more than one best option.)

Worry #1

Worry #2

Worry #3

8. What did you learn from listing your best options in the previous question?

9. Dwelling on the good helps us avoid the worry option and choose one of those other more helpful options. If you were to dwell on the good in each of your worries, what would you dwell on? Be specific, remembering who God is in that situation.

Worry #1

Worry #2

Worry #3

10. What happened when you started listing the good in the midst of your worries?

 PRAYER

11. Read the passage again with your worries in mind, then spend some time visiting with God about them. Ask Him for the outcome you want, but then thank Him for all the good you saw as you thought of the ways He has already blessed you. Ask Him to give you wisdom about any actions He wants you to take and the strength to carry out those actions.

 **TAKEAWAY**

12. What was your biggest takeaway from today's lesson?

 ACTION STEPS

13. List any action steps you'd like to take based on your takeaway.

Chapter 15 Footnotes

22. Proverbs 3:5–6; Luke 10:40–42; Philippians 4:6; 1 Peter 5:7.

23. I know you defined worry in the last chapter, but I think it's helpful to define it again here to see how it compares with our other choices.

SIXTEEN

Learning To Be Content

PHILIPPIANS 4:10–23

10 I rejoiced in the Lord greatly that now at length you have revived your concern for me. You were indeed concerned for me, but you had no opportunity. 11 Not that I am speaking of being in need, for I have learned in whatever situation I am to be content. 12 I know how to be brought low, and I know how to abound. In any and every circumstance, I have learned the secret of facing plenty and hunger, abundance and need. 13 I can do all things through him who strengthens me. 14 Yet it was kind of you to share my trouble. 15 And you Philippians yourselves know that in the beginning of the gospel, when I left Macedonia, no church entered into partnership with me in giving and receiving, except you only. 16 Even in Thessalonica you sent me help for my needs once and again. 17 Not that I seek the gift, but I seek the fruit that increases to your credit. 18 I have received full payment, and more. I am well supplied, having received from Epaphroditus the gifts you sent, a fragrant offering, a sacrifice acceptable and pleasing to God. 19 And my God will supply every need of yours according to his riches in glory in Christ Jesus. 20 To our God and Father be glory forever and ever. Amen. 21 Greet every saint in Christ Jesus. The brothers who are with me greet you. 22 All the saints greet you, especially those of Caesar's household. 23 The grace of the Lord Jesus Christ be with your spirit.

 **OBSERVE**

1. Summarize or diagram this passage.

 **THINK**

2. In this passage Paul talks about the secret of being content. How would you define *content*? How would you define *discontent*?

Content

Discontent

Paul tells us that the secret to contentment is that we can do all things through Christ who strengthens us. Yet, for most of us, the secret is something else: fun, friends, a great job, good health, all of our loved ones doing well, financial security, or any number of things. We feel we can't be content if one of those areas is lacking. Let's see what this looks like in real life.

3. List two or three situations that are currently making you discontent.

4. What do you feel needs to happen in those situations for you to be content?

5. How does your secret to being content (question 4) differ from Paul's secret to being content (v. 13)?

The secret to contentment is to make God our Number One[24] and go to Him for strengthening[25] when we're not getting the other things we want (see question 4). The more we hold everything we have and want with open hands, willing to give them up, if necessary, the more content we'll be.

That doesn't mean we can't act to make life better, though, and often God *wants* us to act. For example, let's say I'm discontent because I'm worried about finances. I need to believe that God will meet my needs just as He said He would,[26] and I need to believe at the gut level that life is about loving God and others (which I can do at any income level), not about being financially secure or having a fun lifestyle. But God might also want me to *act* by budgeting and exploring ways to generate income or cut expenses.

With other worries—such as what will happen in the world—I may not have a lot of options in the action department, but I could still act by buying a journal, recording five things I'm thankful for each day, and praying for the world.

6. What would it look like on a practical level to apply Paul's secret of contentment in Philippians 4:13 to one or two of the areas you mentioned in question 3? What would you believe and how would you act? Be specific.

Believe

Act

When I read Philippians 4:13, I usually focus on the first part of that verse—I can do all things through Jesus—but not so much on the second half—who strengthens me. But here's the thing: I don't get the promise in the first half of the verse unless I go to Jesus so He can do the second part. Let's explore this idea by looking at a type of strengthening we're more familiar with—working out at the gym.

7. Pretend you hate working out and you lack the discipline to make yourself do it (you may not need to pretend!). Now imagine that you've made a New Year's resolution to go to the gym every day for three months. So you hire a trainer and get to work on your goal. Would you expect to get strong in the first week? If not, what would the growth process look like, and what would you have to do to keep getting stronger?

8. What is the trainer's role in the strengthening process? What is your role?

Trainer's role

Your role

9. The thing is, we have a Trainer available for free in real life. Jesus wants to walk alongside us, share His expertise, encourage us, and help us grow through the trials that make us feel discontent (Matthew 11:28–30; Hebrews 4:15–16). Think of the situations you mentioned in question 3. What would it look like to go to Jesus for strengthening so you can learn to be content in those situations? (Review your answer to the previous question if you need ideas.)

If we walk with Jesus, we'll be strengthened. He'll teach us how to be content in the midst of our struggles. If we don't walk with Him, we'll have a hard time feeling content and we'll also miss out on the growth He offers. James 1:2–4 says that God uses our trials to help us grow.

10. In what practical ways do you think God wants you to grow through the situation you mentioned in question 3?

11. Just as the trainer at the gym tells us which weights to lift and how often to lift them, Jesus also gives us practical exercises to strengthen our contentment muscles—Paul shared two of those exercises in Philippians: praying with thanksgiving[27] and dwelling on the good.[28] Why don't you take some time to do one of those exercises right now? Think of the situation you mentioned in question 3 and use one of those exercises to go to Jesus for strengthening. Record your feelings after doing that exercise.

PRAYER

12. Read today's passage again, then spend some time visiting with your Trainer about the situation that's making you discontent. Ask Him for wisdom to handle this situation going forward, strength to do anything He wants you to do, and grace to accept anything you need to accept.

TAKEAWAY

13. What was your biggest takeaway from today's lesson?

ACTION STEPS

14. List any action steps you'd like to take based on your takeaway.

Chapter 16 Footnotes

24. Philippians 3:7–8.
25. Philippians 4:13.
26. Philippians 4:19.
27. Philippians 4:6 and Lesson 14.
28. Philippians 4:8 and Lesson 15.

About Barb Raveling

BARB RAVELING is the author of nine books and Bible studies. Her top-ranked podcasts, *Taste for Truth* and the *Christian Habits Podcast,* have earned over a million downloads and continue to inspire people to break free from their strongholds and grow closer to God. Barb's passion is teaching people how to renew their minds so they can experience transformation. She writes and teaches from her own experience of renewing her mind for the last twenty-plus years as well as her experience as a certified executive Christian coach with extensive training in biblical counseling. You can connect with Barb on Instagram, YouTube, or through her website at barbraveling.com.

Other Books by Barb Raveling

Say Goodbye to Emotional Eating

James (Closer to God Bible Study Series)

Freedom from Procrastination Bible Study

Rally: A Bible Study on Trials

Renewing of the Mind Project

Taste for Truth Weight Loss Bible Study

I Deserve a Donut (and Other Lies That Make You Eat)

Freedom from Emotional Eating Bible Study

Barb's Podcasts

Christian Habits Podcast

Taste for Truth Podcast